Vivid Visualisation™

Success without Stress!

John Freeman

Rubbish Love Publishing (Gibraltar) 2016

Table of Contents

Your Free recordings

To get your ten 5 minute (ish) visualisation recordings please copy the link below into your browser. They are in MP3 format, so just download them to your computer and copy them to your music player. Each recording is designed to be listened to 'on the run'. That's to say you can carry them with you and listen any time you need five minutes peace and quiet. For best results pick one and stick to it for a month or so.

Please be aware: The recordings are for the express purposes of listening to with *eyes closed*. They are NOT to be listened to whilst driving or operating machinery.

These recordings are meant solely for the readers of this book.

I accept no responsibility for anything that arises from their use.

http://johnfreeman-stressbuster.com/ten-free-recordings/

INTRODUCTION

Do you find life a struggle? Do you try to achieve things but never seem to accomplish them? Do you ever set goals but not know how to make them happen?

If you are feeling frustrated, stuck or just plain sick of getting nowhere, this book is for you. Likewise, if you have read about the law of attraction but you are still not seeing results, then you are about to gain a great deal of insight.

Whatever you want from life, whatever it is that you are trying to achieve, will be a hell of a lot easier when you build, and hold, a powerful vision of it in your imagination first. In fact, without this type of visualisation, getting what you want will always be a struggle. Frustration, struggle and self-doubt are all results of not having a powerful enough vision to pull us towards what we want.

The vision we hold for ourselves is the target our subconscious mind is constantly and consistently aiming at. Many of us even hold a negative vision of what we *don't* want that actively pulls us in the opposite direction of our dreams. As a result, we wonder why life is so difficult, and why we keep moving farther and farther away from our goals. If you have ever desperately tried to achieve something but didn't get anywhere, you will know exactly what this feels like.

What you are about to discover is my step-by-step system for getting what you want. I'll teach you how to stop struggling and take charge of your life. I will show you how to sit back, relax, and create the life you want. Without stress, worry, or even hard work.

While that may sound impossible, it is actually truly achievable. By the time you finish reading this book, you will be able to accomplish anything you want, anytime you want. You are going to be a master of visualisation, a champion of creation, and you will be well on your way to creating a whole new world for yourself.

Visualisation really works! But it absolutely has to be done right. Once you can do it properly, things will begin to fall into place for you. You will put an end to your struggling and improve the quality and quantity of results in all of your endeavours. With Vivid Visualisation™ you will transform every area of your life.

It is so easy too! I will guide you carefully through each step of the process. First I will explain how and why visualisation works. You will see that not only are you capable of visualising but you are already doing it—all day, every day. You will learn what a powerful visualisation should look like, what it should feel like, and what elements your vision should contain. You will amass all the tools you need to unleash the immense power of your subconscious and make it work for you in the most amazing way.

Finally, I will help you create deep, uncompromising happiness that can withstand all of life's trials. And all you have to do is sit in your armchair and get comfy.

What could be easier than that?

Who am I?

And how am I qualified to teach you how to visualise?

My name is John Freeman, and I am an Advanced Hypnotherapist, and a Vision Coach, specialising in helping frustrated people move towards their goals in a motivated and inspired way. I have been influencing the subconscious mind of my clients for over fifteen years, getting them "unstuck" so they can build and maintain happy lives of fulfilment.

I am also the creator of Vivid Visualisations™, personalised hypnosis and meditation recordings designed to connect in a powerful way to the deepest part of the listener. They are completely unique in the world today. I make them intuitively; one take, no script, "*direct from my subconscious to yours*".

Every word and sentence is crafted in my subconscious mind with the intention of connecting deeply with the subconscious mind of the listener. The visualisations I create help my clients make deep and lasting changes. My recordings have helped hundreds of people live simpler, more satisfying lives.

In short, I create visualisations for a living!

Done, properly, frequently, and for long enough, visualisation will rock your world. You can have anything you want. You can reach your goals. You can be happy. You can have money. You can find love. You can be successful. And you can do it all easily, calmly, and carefree.

THE POWER OF CREATION

The infinite intelligence that created everything is inherent within every cell of your body. Without doubt, everything we know in space and time was created by an intelligence. I'm not saying it is a conscious intelligence—I don't know if it is or not—but it is definitely an intelligence. It's the same intelligence that turns an acorn into an oak, that holds us to the Earth with gravity, that created this beautiful planet, that created *you*.

So let's think about you for a minute. That intelligence, whatever it is, created you, so that intelligence has to be *in* you. How could it not? You began life as nothing more than an egg and a sperm. These two tiny cells hold all the information needed for *everything* you will ever think, be, or do. As the two cells become one and then begin to split, each and every new cell knows exactly where to go, what to do, and how to communicate with the others. Each and every cell feels everything you feel, and each and every cell has the ability to heal itself.

Think about a simple cut. It bleeds, it scabs, and it heals. You break a bone—it sets, it grows back together, and it heals. Now think about something as simple as picking up a cup of tea. Do you consciously operate the muscles needed to move your arm, hand, and fingers to grip the cup? What about when you actually drink it? Do you actively operate the swallowing mechanisms? Don't even get me started on the digestive system, the vascular system, the organs, the skeleton, and all the perfectly synchronised bits and pieces that keep you upright, functioning, and mobile all day long, all *life*long.

You, my friend, are a walking, talking miracle. As far as we know, you are the greatest, most exciting, most incredible creation in the entire universe. Yes, you! You are alive, and you have conscious thought. Pause for a minute and think about that.

Life. That, surely, is the biggest miracle. You are no more or no less than anyone else. Yes, lovely, adorable you. A living, breathing miracle of creation.

Now, get this: that intelligence we just talked about lives within every molecule of you. That means all of that creative power is within you. All that is, all that can be, all that we haven't even begun to think of yet—it is *all* within you. God lives within you, and you have that creative power within you to use in any way you please.

I believe that every human being is created with the same capabilities that the intelligence that created us possesses. I believe we have as much creative ability as we choose to embrace, develop, and use. I believe that one day, maybe not for a thousand years, there will be some of us who will leave this planet by our own force of will, choose a space out there in the cosmos, and create a living, breathing thing all of our own. We will then sit back and watch in astonishment and wonder as it grows and evolves into something amazing and wonderful. We will create a life like ourselves—in our own image—that is conscious and can make choices. We will weep at their mistakes and glow with joy and pride as they manage to overcome, grow, and learn from their experiences.

But before we get too carried away with that adventure, let's focus on creating a wonderful, beautiful world of our own right here and right now. Let's create happiness for ourselves, and focus on generating some good in our lives. Let's create some successes in our own world first.

In the grand scheme of all the amazing and wonderful stuff that has been created throughout the universe, you creating the life you want can't be that difficult, can it?

The subconscious vs. The conscious mind

When I talk about the subconscious mind, I am not just talking about a part of your brain. I am talking about that infinite intelligence that is inherent within every cell of your body.

Imagine an iceberg. The 10 percent of the structure that's above the water is your conscious mind, and the remaining 90 percent lying beneath the surface is the all-powerful subconscious mind. As far as we are concerned, the conscious mind, on the surface, has only one job: to choose, to decide *what* you want. The subconscious mind, beneath the surface, uncovers *how* to achieve what you want. It is the creative mind. The subconscious mind has access to all the knowledge that ever was, ever is, and ever will be.

The struggle in our lives is so often caused by us trying to use the conscious mind to either change what we don't want or create what we do want. The trouble with this approach is that our conscious mind doesn't know the answer. Our conscious mind doesn't know *how.*

Our conscious mind is simply *not capable* of creation.

When we try to create with our conscious mind, we make things very difficult for ourselves. Instead, we end up creating a variety of negative energies and emotions, such as:

- Stress

- Struggle

- Pain

- Anger

- Frustration

- Worry

- Anxiety

- Depression

- Loneliness

- Failure

Think about how often you get stuck not knowing what to do. How many times have you changed your mind about what you want because you can't figure out how to get it?

Most of the trouble we have with being who we want to be, and having what we want, comes from trying to work out the *how* with the part of our mind that was never designed for that type of creativity. The only job for the conscious mind is to choose. It doesn't know *how*, so don't waste any more time trying to work it all out with that part of you. Let it go. Hand it over to the part of you that does know—the subconscious.

The subconscious *always* knows *how*. It knows the best way, the quickest way, the easiest way. We can trust this innate power to create what we want and make life easy for ourselves, or we can ignore it and continue to struggle. This deeper intelligence within us is connected to all that is known and all that is yet undiscovered. We can recognise this amazing power and use it to our advantage, Or by default, we can spend our lives worrying, imagining and expecting the worst, hating ourselves, and filling our minds with self-doubt.

The massive intelligence of the subconscious mind has but one job. That is to do everything in its power to help you. I could write a whole book on how powerful the subconscious is and what it is capable of doing in order to deliver what it thinks you want.

For example, my own subconscious created acute pancreatitis within me because it knew I wanted to stop drinking but I wasn't doing anything about it. The result was seven days in hospital and a ban on drinking alcohol because that was the *cause* of the pancreatitis. I had a few little drinks a couple of years later over Christmas and, sure enough, it came back. No more drinking for me, I can tell you! I am a much happier and healthier man because of it, too. That was just one of the ways my subconscious mind has looked after me in the best way it knew how.

The underlying causes of our problems

In the example above, I had a need that I wasn't acknowledging—to give up drinking and hanging around the pub all the time. I knew that life had so much more to offer. On the surface, I was denying this deep, inner truth. I was ignoring my soul's desire. I was pushing it down and continuing to do the thing that was making me, at the deepest level, unhappy.

Our subconscious is truly our best friend. In this instance, as in many others, that inner intelligence found a way to look after me and give me what I wanted.

I wasn't doing it, so my subconscious did it for me!

Another example you may relate to more easily is when you start day dreaming whilst driving your car, and you suddenly realise you are way down the road and don't remember driving the last few miles. That was your subconscious taking care of you, and driving the car while you were distracted.

Secondary Gains

As human beings, we are full of deeply buried needs and desires. These feelings, that we might have denied to ourselves for years because they are too painful to face, are being met by the power of the subconscious mind every day. These deeply buried needs can be rounded up into six categories called secondary gains.

There are six main secondary gains: Attention, Protection, Punishment (of ourselves or others), Manipulation, Avoidance, and Importance. Whenever there is a negative in your life, your subconscious will be meeting at least one of these hidden needs. In the case of my pancreatitis, it was avoidance. I wanted more from life than hanging around in pubs and getting drunk all the time. But for one reason or another, I wasn't doing anything about it, so my subconscious took control and did it for me.

Even after decades of healing work on myself, I can still get aches and pains, or feel poorly because of a childhood need for importance and attention.

Your subconscious is always giving you what it thinks you want and need. The deeper you bury your truth, the more the subconscious will take charge of it! [*remember I said that later when I talk about how well and how often you need to visualise!*] In order to achieve this, it can and does create behaviours and/or physical conditions. It will also attract any circumstances or people that it thinks you need. Believe me, this is easy stuff for the power that creates life.

Whatever problem you have, be it with yourself or others, *look to yourself.* When you look for what you might be gaining from that problem you can begin to heal or change it. This kind of introspection is not easy, but it's always well worth the effort.

Reprogramming ourselves

The subconscious mind is being programmed all day every day in regards to what you want. The feelings you feel *are* that programming. More importantly, from a parenting perspective, the feelings you create in your children are their programming. Spend your time creating good feelings in your child and you will raise a well balanced, confident, happy person.

If you had an excess of bad feelings as a child yourself, then that was your own negative programming which your subconscious is using today as its guidance system. Even if you deny that you feel a certain way, your subconscious will set about answering the needs related to those feelings. The only way to change that programming is to change how you feel.

The best way to do that is for you to visualise purposefully what you want and to create the feelings associated with your vision. The subconscious is then redirected towards what you want and away from what you don't want. The more frequent, intense, vivid, and deeply embedded these visualisations become, the quicker and more easily your subconscious gets to work on them for you. It's the same concept you use when teaching a child how to spell a word. If you simply tell him how to spell it once, he may forget tomorrow and go back to spelling it the wrong way again. But if you get him to practise it over and over, it becomes embedded in his psyche.

The job of your conscious mind is to choose what those visualisations are to be, and to make them strong, powerful, and intense. You need to focus on those images frequently, persistently, and resolutely until the subconscious can be sure you are not going to change your mind again, and it can then attract it, create it, or drive you passionately and effortlessly towards it.

If you fail to take charge of this power within, if you choose not to feed it positive images of what you want, it will act on the images of what you *don't* want. Your deepest fears, your biggest worries, your insecurities, your lack of self-love and approval—all will be created easily and effortlessly over and over again.

Until you wake up!

Let today be the day that you choose to control this immense intelligence. Let today be the day you begin directing it towards who you want to be and what you want to have.

WHAT IS VISUALISATION?

The simplest and most powerful way to communicate what we want to this powerful, all-creating force is with pictures, images in the mind's eye.

Imagination *equals* images

Visualisation, therefore, is the deliberate use of vivid, memorable images to create the feelings associated with anything you want.

Visualisation is simply the art of using your imagination in a purposeful, positive way to program your subconscious with what you want—to give your subconscious its directional guidance. We can all do it. We were born with this gift, and when we take charge of it we can create incredible things. With visualisation, there is no need to push against the tide, no need to struggle, and most importantly, no need to know *how* we are going to achieve what we want.

I can promise you this: the more you let go of the *how's* and trust that a way will be found, and the more you begin engaging the power of your subconscious, the quicker and more easily your dream will be realised. Believe me, nothing has ever been created without someone somewhere seeing it in his or her mind's eye first.

Albert Einstein riding on a beam of light.

Thomas Edison seeing in the dark.

Henry Ford and the Model T.

NASA going to the moon.

The Wright brothers taking to the air.

Apple. Microsoft. Google. Facebook. Amazon. Bridges. Buildings. Wheels. Airplanes. Super Tankers. Televisions. Telephones. The Internet. *Everything*, big or small, was first imagined in the mind's eye of the creator.

You see, religion talks about the creator creating the world, but we humans create our own world, and we have been doing it ever since we got here. You too can create your own world. And you do—every day. But if you don't take charge of creating a *positive* world for yourself, you will create a negative world by default.

When we talk about our problems, even when we think about them, we give them power. We feed them. Have you heard about the two wolves that live within you? There is the happy, fulfilled wolf and the sad, frustrated wolf. The stronger of the two is whichever one you feed.

Whatever is crappy about your life must be ignored to the best of your ability. I know it is a hard thing to do, but it is not impossible and you don't have to do it nonstop. Just at intervals throughout your day, that's all.

The reality of today is merely what was created yesterday. The real secret to a happy life is to shift your focus away from what you don't like and use your imagination to create the feelings of what you do like. Anything you can think of can be created in the imagination; and if it can be created in the imagination, it can be created in reality too.

There is no doubt about it, you are the creator of your own world, so what are you choosing to create today? As Esther Hicks and Abraham say, "Nothing you want is upstream." That means that if you think about what makes you *unhappy*, you can't have what makes you *happy*! If what you are doing feels like a struggle, there is no way it can be helping you get what you want. No way!

You just have to trust that the answers you seek are available to you. Stop struggling, and instead use your imagination to take yourself where you want to go. Take charge and live life purposefully. Honestly, that is all it takes. The more you let go of the worry and stress, and the more you let go of the *how*, the quicker and easier your subconscious will start to make the good stuff happen for you.

Stress, struggle, worry, frustration, and self-doubt, are all solid blocks to the creative process. Get out of your own way. Stop fighting yourself. Instead of struggling on the outside, put all of your effort into creating positive images on the inside. You are the creator, and visualisation is your primary tool for the job.

How often do you need to visualise the things you want?

The real beauty of visualisation is that once you have done it a couple of times properly—and I mean, of course, vividly—the image should be so powerful that it will just keep popping into your head all day long. That is when the magic starts to happen. That is when you begin creating who you want to be, and what you want to have.

Use visualisation to keep you focused and moving forward. Use your visualisations to draw all that you desire into your life. No matter what is happening around you or to you, once you begin using your imagination in this way you are free. You can be anything. You can do anything. You can have anything.

Whilst you are living in your imagination, the feelings you create are as real to your subconscious as anything outside of you. When you use your imagination to the extent that you can feel what you want is real, the subconscious cannot tell that it is only in your mind. It is as real as real life is real.

It is real because you feel it, and the only thing that ever matters is how you feel. When you create these wonderful, amazing feelings of what you want, they are real. When you feel them, they are real. Feelings are real. Feelings are the *only* things that are real. And once you feel it, you own it. It is yours. It belongs to you. Nobody can take it away. And the more you feel it, the closer you are to creating it in reality.

So what is the answer to the question, how often should you visualise?

As often as you need to in order to create the feeling of already having what you want. As often as it takes, for as long as it takes. Just keep building your vision. When you get frustrated because things don't go your way, take a breath and visualise what you want again. When a problem arises, step back from it and visualise the desired result instead. When you get stressed about something, stop, breath, and visualise what you want.

The more often you create the feelings of what you want, the quicker your reality will match your imagination.

HOW TO GET STARTED

Make a decision

A guy walks into a railway station and casually goes up to the counter.

"Can I have a ticket please?" he asks the man behind the counter.

The man frowns but in a friendly voice asks, "Where to, son?"

The guy shrugs. "I dunno, mate."

"Well if you don't know, how can I sell you a ticket?" the man points out. "Best you go over there and sit on that bench. Come back and see me when you make your mind up where you want to go."

When I was twenty-eight years old I went to work for the Combined Insurance Company of America (C.I.C.A.). It was owned by a guy called W. Clement Stone. The first thing the company did when you arrived for training was to give you a couple of books written by the man himself: *The Success System that Never Fails,* and *Success Through a Positive Mental Attitude.*

Now, bearing in mind that I was twenty-eight at the time, this was the first I had ever heard that there were such things as positive and negative attitudes. I had been one hundred percent negative about virtually everything in my life up until that time, and I thought this newfangled positive-attitude thing was brilliant. I devoured the book.

"I am a positive thinker. I'm going to be rich and successful!" I would declare to everyone who would listen. I thought I had found the Holy Grail. I thought everything was going to change. I thought all my misery, loneliness, and worthlessness was over. I thought wrong.

Despite reading a ton of self-help books over the next twenty or so years, listening to the tapes, going to the seminars, even training as a hypnotherapist, I stayed negative. I made improvements, but my progress was painful and snail-paced.

I started my own business, and I worked my arse off. Nobody in the world worked as hard as I did. But all I managed to do was struggle. In all those years, do you know what I created for myself? It wasn't success or riches, I can tell you. All I created was stress, frustration, anxiety, worry, and exhaustion.

There was certainly no prosperity, very little calm, and I was even bankrupt at one time. I helped hundreds of people with my hypnotherapy, whilst simultaneously spinning my wheels and making no meaningful progress for myself.

So what was wrong?

Well, for a start, being positive takes an awful lot of effort, and truthfully, I wasn't making anywhere near enough. But mainly, all my efforts were being spent outwardly on struggling to make things happen in the physical world.

The first thing you need to know is that *success begins on the inside*. I read that at the beginning of my foray into self-help books, maybe it was even in one of W. Clement Stone's books. But it took me over two decades to *get it*. That sentence now lies at the heart of this book.

Success begins on the inside.

I shall quantify that even further.

Success begins (or ends) in your own imagination.

The whole point of this book is to get you to stop struggling all the time, busting your gut, swimming against the tide, crawling uphill, or spinning your wheels achieving nothing, the way I was. All your hard work should go into creating what you want on the inside first. I urge you to stop doing anything right now that is causing you worry or frustration. Don't waste another minute of your time feeling frustrated. Instead, let it go and retreat into your all-powerful imagination and recreate your reality into what you want it to be.

I don't mean live there. I just mean visit often.

That is the one thing I didn't do in all those years of struggling for "success". I had no vision for myself. I was so busy *doing* stuff that I didn't have time to *create* stuff. I simply ran around like a headless chicken. Busy, busy, busy. Running away from what I didn't want.

No vision. No purpose. No success. What a complete and utter waste of time. All that wasted energy. All that wasted effort. In a quarter of a century I achieved nothing of any worth. The only value that came out of those experiences were the lessons I learnt, and that I now share to encourage you not to make the same mistakes.

The problem was that "striving for success" was way too vague. Actually, as I look back now, I can see that "striving for success" was actually my true goal. And, of course, I achieved my true goal every day. Without a consciously chosen, specific, measurable goal for my subconscious to lock onto, it just ensured that I got what it thought I wanted. Striving, more striving, and then even more striving.

I didn't *decide* on anything. I didn't define what success was. What did it mean to me? I had no idea. If a successful man had asked me how he could help me, I would have embarrassed myself. I didn't even know how he could help me. What could I have said?

"Duh, I dunno, lend me some money to pay my bills, maybe?"

You have to *decide*! You have to choose something. Anything. Just pick something that you can focus your energy on and start creating. During those wasted decades, I used to change my mind every other day about what I wanted. I could never make up my mind. I had no trust, no faith; in myself or a higher power.

It's very different now, though. Now I know exactly what I want, when I want it, and even what I want *after* that. And no, I don't know *how* most of it is coming. But I do know that it's coming. I know because I can see it, I can *feel* it. Because the vision inside me grows bigger, louder, and brighter every day. It does this because I decided. I finally chose something, and I stick with it on the inside, no matter what. No matter what happens outside, I stay the course *inside*. This gives me the opportunity to nurture my vision, to tend it and care for it. Expand it. Feel it breath and live within me.

Because of this powerful vision I am always assured that I am moving in the right direction, making the correct choices, and my dreams are getting closer to reality.

But you can only do that if you decide what you want and stick with it through everything the world throws at you. Furthermore, you will only create it outside once you have built that vision strongly enough on the inside anyway.

You see? You have to put in the effort to create what you want on the inside first. You *have* to!

Hypnotherapy has proved many, many times how amazingly effective it is for creating deep and lasting changes for people. But at the end of the day, all the hypnotherapist is working towards is to get a client to *decide* the problem will go, change, end, whatever. The hypnotherapist and the client might have do all sorts of work together to get to that point, but sooner or later, the client has to *decide*. Because after that decision is made, nothing in the world can prevent the all-powerful subconscious from creating the desired change.

I have seen this happen hundreds of times; for transforming anxiety, stress, negative habits, physical ailments, and all sorts of issues and problems.

Within the human race, everything that has ever been achieved began with someone somewhere making a decision. No ifs, no buts. If you *try* to give up smoking, that is all you will ever do. If you *try* to lose weight, that is all you will ever do. If you *try* to be successful, that is all you will ever do. All you will ever do is *try*.

Great things begin to happen in your life when you *decide* they will happen. Amazing things occur to help you on your way after you choose to make something happen. Everything begins for you today. Forget what's in the past. Every day is a new beginning. Let today be yours.

Don't be like that guy in the train station, who is surely still sitting on that bench today, still thinking about what he wants out of life, still trying to make up his mind, still trying to make one, powerful, definite decision that will take him to a new adventure.

The fact is, the easiest way to stay stuck is to never decide to go anywhere. The easiest way to make something happen is to decide it will, and tell yourself that nothing in the world is going to stop you.

So first things first . . .

For God's sake, *pick something*. One thing. Big or small, it doesn't matter. What matters is that you make a choice. Forget about *how* it will come about. Just pick something and pick it now.

You might have a bill to pay, a perfect job to get, a new partner to attract, or a home to buy. Maybe you want to change the world. Maybe you just want to tidy up the garden. Just pick one thing right now and decide that you will use the techniques in this book to create it. No matter what happens on the outside, make a commitment to yourself to continue building a new vision for yourself on the inside. Decide that nothing will change your mind, that you will stay the course, and it will come about no matter what.

You know that thing that happens when you buy a new car? You start to see the same car everywhere, don't you? That's focus. That's laser sharp focus created by the subconscious mind because you drew attention to a specific type of car.

So decide on something now, and begin to create that thing in your imagination. Begin to engage the laser sharp focus of your subconscious mind.

Start living, and enjoying, a purpose driven life!

Use a scale of percentages

Now is the time to be really honest with yourself. Think about the thing you have decided on and think of a scale of percentages—zero per cent to 100 per cent—and ask yourself these questions:

Where on that scale are your feelings in relation to what you want? How far away from what you want are you emotionally?

Just close your eyes and imagine the scale. Ask the questions, and trust what your subconscious tells you or shows you. Your answers to these questions will give you a powerful starting point, and you can begin building your vision from there. No matter where you are on the scale, it is important to know the reality. Because with what you are about to learn, you can begin to power up the scale toward 100 percent as if you have a rocket up your arse.

Let's start getting you thinking in pictures.

Close your eyes and imagine your percentage scale. Picture your scale in your favourite colours. In relation to your goal, see where you are, and see where you are going. Paint a great big, colourful picture of yourself enjoying the end result at the top of your scale. Hear people congratulating you there. Turn the volume up. Turn up the brightness, the colour. Add movement. Add fireworks. Trumpets. Make reaching 100 per cent as spectacular as you can possibly make it. Make it so irresistible that you are drawn to it as if your scale is a traction beam, pulling you ever closer to your dream result. Eyes on the prize, always. And finally, see yourself shooting up that scale like Superman (or woman)!

That's a pretty simple version of a really effective visualisation. Use it as a basis for your own visualisation. See yourself where you are, see the end result all lit up, see yourself flying towards it, and see yourself actually getting there. Feel what it feels like to arrive. Simple.

You need to practise building that image every day. The more you imagine it, the higher up the scale you move. The higher up the scale you move internally, the closer to your goal you get in reality. Your goal is to climb your scale in your own imagination. Leave the rest for your subconscious to figure out.

Each time you return to this exercise you will find that you begin at a slightly higher percentage than you were the last time. I promise you that by the time you reach the 70 per cent point in your imagination, you will begin to smell it and taste it. You will know by then where it is coming from, how it is coming, what you have to do to get it, *and* you will be enjoying the inspired actions you are taking. Your goal and your pursuit of it will have become fun.

Now get this . . . At precisely the moment when you reach 100 per cent on the scale in your imagination, you will have achieved it in reality as well. When you can no longer tell the difference between what you imagine and what is outside of you, that is the moment of creation.

That is the Big Bang!

Build your vision on the inside to make it happen on the outside. That is the law of attraction. That is how to stop struggling and get what you want. Know where you are on that percentage scale, and begin lifting yourself up the scale with a powerful vision for yourself. The rest takes care of itself as the following miracles begin to occur in your life in ever-growing frequency:

- Inspiration

- Motivation

- Good luck

- Serendipity

- Creativity

- Even more motivation

- Golden opportunities

Each of these things, in turn, will help you to make your vision even stronger. Developing a positive cycle of creation and forward momentum which will simply blow you away.

Focus on 10 percent at a time

If you are a very long way away from what you want, I know that big vision of 100 per cent might seem too far away right now. The further away it is on that scale, the harder it will be for you to create the feelings of having it. This, I believe, is the single most common reason why people don't make this stuff work. It is just too hard to imagine what they want because they have to reach too far up the scale. Then they give up because they can't see, or feel, themselves where they want to be.

Keep practising your big vision two or three times a day. Always use the same vision, building, improving, and nurturing it. Think of anything you have accomplished in the past—learning to walk, riding a bike, anything. You always have to practise before it comes naturally. It is no different with visualisation. Practise this and get it right, and you can take the difficulty out of achieving anything you want.

But as you practise visualising your big vision more often, also spend time focusing on raising yourself the next 10 per cent. Or even 5 per cent if that works better for you. That might mean the next bill paid or even just some money put aside for it, or the next half a stone in weight lost, or five cigarettes fewer smoked each day, another paying customer, or even just to meet and say hello to more people you like.

You will find it so much easier to imagine a smaller increase. It will be easier to picture, easier to imagine, easier to change your feelings. Remember, it is all about the feelings, so just keep reaching for what is just out of reach. This, of course, will give you more successes to celebrate and feel good about.

Take your vision from wide to narrow

You might find that when you first start to create something, your vision may not be too specific. That is OK. Things will get clearer for you as you keep visualising and taking action. As long as you know which direction you are going in and begin moving.

I once had a general vision of myself being a coach. With persistence and determination, that vision gradually became this book, my website, my blog, my clients, all sorts. Even while I was writing this book, the vision was constantly narrowing with regards to what services I wanted to provide and who I wanted to work with. This was because I continually kept building that vision, filling in the blanks, and taking the actions that moved me towards what I wanted. My vision for myself kept becoming more and more detailed with constant practise.

As you take the necessary actions to move yourself closer to what you want you become more inspired and more creative, your vision will narrow as mine did, becoming far more precise. I can now see and feel, *without any effort,* exactly what lies before me for the next year, and beyond. Everything is as clear as can be. Each area has narrowed down to such a precise laser beam of focus that I hardly make any effort at all. Seriously, I just can't stop visualising what I want now. That is not to say I am not working hard. I work longer hours at the moment than I ever have worked before. But it is *inspired action.*

Visualising properly has given me clarity, purpose, fulfilment, energy, vitality, joy, happiness, and inner peace. I'm not kidding. I genuinely feel all of those things as I write. I didn't visualise *any* of these things, but they have come to me as an extremely happy side effect of visualising what I wanted, gradually narrowing down my focus and taking inspired action towards what I want.

And the real beauty of this? I could have just visualised myself being any one of those things instead: fulfilment, vitality, joy, happiness; visualising any one of those would have helped me create the same successes I have created. The subconscious always finds a way! So here is a tip for you. If you don't know what you want, just visualise great happiness and joy for yourself. Your subconscious will then set about creating that for you in the most suitable way possible.

It doesn't matter how long you have been doing it wrong either, begin today to do it right. Begin wherever you are and move forward as the inspiration grabs you. If you are not inspired yet, spend more time narrowing down your vision rather than banging your head against a wall.

All the things you currently think are wrong in your life are just life lessons waiting to be learnt. Take a breath and realise what a gift it all is. Every successful man or woman can regale you with stories of the struggle they had before they made it, and I bet every one of them will tell you that they are thankful for all of the lessons they learnt on the way. I know I, for one, would not be where I am today if I had not travelled the path I did.

Decide on what you want, Stay focused on it, visualise it until it feels real, take the inspired actions. Keep repeating until it happens for you.

THE CREATION PROCESS

What are affirmations?

I was using Facebook recently, and as I was scrolling through the comments on a post, I read a comment that said, "I think affirmations are a load of rubbish!" This got me thinking, and I woke up in the early hours reaching for my notebook.

If you were to look in the dictionary the definition would be something like,

Affirmation —the statement of the truth of something.

But this doesn't do this amazing word the justice it deserves. Affirmations are the thoughts we think and feel all day, every day. They represent our deepest held beliefs about ourselves and the world around us. If we pay attention to these thoughts, we can then notice what we really feel and begin to change it.

As such, the *truth* mentioned in the definition above could also be explained as the deepest feelings we have about any given subject. A definition I prefer then, is,

Affirmation —our feelings expressed as words.

Every time you open your mouth to speak, you are affirming how you feel. Your deepest held beliefs and feelings will show up in your attitude towards everything in your life. If you want to change your life, change how you speak—and what you speak of.

The first step in achieving anything in our lives is to adjust how we feel about it. An important way to do that is through affirmations. But they have to be used properly to be effective. People often think affirmations and visualisations don't work simply because they don't use them properly.

With affirmations, as well as visualisations, you have to *feel* them. Feel the words in an affirmation and feel the pictures in a visualisation. You have to! It's always about the feelings. We feel happy, or we feel sad. We feel fat, or we feel thin. We feel successful, or we feel like a failure. We feel rich, or we feel poor. We feel motivated or we feel lazy. And so it goes.

Affirmations are words, that create feelings, that create reality. They are not rubbish; they are a great way to begin the visualisation process.

.

Getting started

Let me say this: remember that this stuff works. Ask any successful person in the world and they will tell you that they could "see" their dreams in their mind's eyes long before they actually achieved their goals. Very often they were the *only* person who could see it. If you do this right, you can have what you want.

You know how powerful the subconscious is, right? You can make as many excuses as you want, but you—and only you—can hold yourself back. You have the power to change your life. Sure, it is tricky at first, but it gets easier. And I know of no easier way to do this than what you are learning right now.

If you think you are making excuses for your lack of commitment, and you really want to get unstuck, find a coach. Find someone you can bond with, who will support, encourage, and guide you. Find someone who believes in you. Find someone you can enter a partnership with, who you can trust to be honest and straightforward with you. You want a coach who will hold you accountable for the commitments you make to yourself and won't let you off the hook or let you make excuses.

Yes, it can be uncomfortable, but it is also hugely satisfying, very exciting, and extremely fulfilling. All the effort we make creating excuses is effort we could put into creating what we want. Everyone who has ever been coached will tell you that it played a huge part in his or her success. Most coaches will even give you a free session to try it out, so why don't you give it a go?

Five Times

This a great little exercise that I created, and have been sharing with my clients, for more than sixteen years now. I like to keep things very simple and uncomplicated, and it doesn't get any simpler than this. And I can promise you it works. I became a non-smoker using this technique many years ago. It is an extremely effective way of developing a creative cycle with your subconscious mind, so let's give it a try.

Remember to do this slowly and take the time to really feel the words as you say them.

No feelings equals no result!

Start by repeating the following statement five times. Say it aloud if possible.

"I feel amazing!"

Say it however it comes to mind. There is no need to be overly fussy about it, as long as your words are based on the above statement and you repeat it *five times*.

Within a short time other positive thoughts about yourself begin to enter your mind, usually within an hour. Every time *any* of these new, positive thoughts enter your head, repeat them *five times* as well. Every time a *negative* thought enters your head, notice it, and replace it with its opposite, positive alternative . . . and repeat it *five times*, of course.

Silence and quiet are not negative so don't need to be filled. Instead, enjoy the peace and harmony they bring to you. Keep your affirmation related to "being" rather than "having." You are creating a self-contained, positive, powerful new belief structure that is *not* based on anything external to yourself (i.e. not "I have a lovely new car," but "I feel amazing!!!").

If at any time you cannot think of an alternative positive affirmation, simply return to the one I wrote for you above and start again. Also return to this original affirmation whenever you become aware that you have slipped into your old pattern of thinking (instead of giving yourself a hard time).

Believe me, the more you commit to this process, the more often you will notice this happening, and the quicker you are able to replace your negative affirmations with your positive affirmations.

Be vigilant! Be persistent! Be determined!

Tell nobody what you are doing. Talking about it takes power and energy away from doing it.

This is a proven method of affecting rapid, positive change, but it only works when you stick with it. So don't give up after a couple of days, or even a couple of weeks. Keep at it *until* you get what you want. You can use other words instead if you prefer: fantastic, lovely, wonderful, terrific. The list of positive adjectives is vast.

Whatever you decide on, keep it short and sweet. I don't like long-winded affirmations, and find them quite ineffective. They drag on too long to create any worthwhile feelings. Short and punchy affirmations are highly effective every time. Stick with the same affirmation for a month. Go on, amaze yourself.

One-word affirmations

Think of your conscious mind as a cynical, old gatekeeper guarding the subconscious. He doesn't want to believe all the good things you tell yourself, so if anything is too far off of what he believes to be true, he will block it before it gets to that precious realm of the subconscious.

The great secret to programming the subconscious (which believes anything we tell it) is simply to get past the gatekeeper.

When we use affirmations, we can cut a huge corner by simply saying—and feeling—single words. It is much easier to sneak past the gatekeeper with just one word, rather than a full statement. Remember, the subconscious believes everything, but the conscious mind is far more cynical.

If I tell myself, "I'm the sexiest man alive!", my conscious mind, the gatekeeper, says, "No you're not, you silly twerp." And slams the gate shut in my face.

But if I just repeat, "Sexy!" over and over again, the nasty old gatekeeper doesn't notice a contradiction to what he believes. Then he doesn't notice me sneaking through the gate.

So pick one positive adjective that resonates with you and try it out for a few weeks. Use it as a mantra. This one word, repeated often, will embed itself within your subconscious and eventually become a feeling—if you stick with it long enough!

How long is enough? As long as it takes!

GUIDANCE FOR EFFECTIVE VISUALISATION

1. ***The more relaxed you are, the more effective visualisation will be.***

A hypnotherapist relaxes you in order for your (gate keeper) conscious mind to get distracted and the subconscious to come to the surface. In this way, the subconscious, which believes anything it is told, takes on board the images and suggestions, and automatically believes them to be true. When you get back into a wide awake state again, your subconscious returns to the depth of your being and takes the newly introduced feelings with it. These positive feelings, in turn, become a part of your very existence.

Your subconscious then sets about producing the behaviours and circumstances that match the new feelings. You become what you are visualising yourself to be because you have done enough with your visualisations to make the deeper, powerful, inner you believe that your vision is true. And all you had to do was imagine it was so!

So take your time. Relax. Breath. Let go. If all you have to do is relax and use your imagination, surely it is worth doing it right?

As each visualisation becomes more deeply ingrained in your subconscious, you can do it anywhere, anytime. But for now, take your time and get relaxed first. The absolute best time to do this is as you are falling asleep and first thing when you wake up. This is when your gatekeeper is not paying so much attention and your subconscious is naturally close to the surface and ready, willing, and able to assimilate your positive instructions.

Begin and end your day the successful way!

2. ***Start with my examples, and then allow your own visualisations to grow out of them.***

Begin by following the instructions and using the examples I give you here. But as you use them, they will begin to morph. They will take on their own life and become more meaningful to you. I do a hypnosis recording that guides my clients to walk down some steps into a beautiful garden. After a few weeks of listening to it, my clients would invent caves, paddling pools, and God knows what else halfway down. They would ask me if that was all right, and I always said, "Of course!" If it comes from your own subconscious, it will resonate even better within your Subconscious. And if you can resonate with something, you can have it, be it, or do it.

I love that word. *Resonate.* Get your visualisation to resonate within you. As you begin to resonate with what you want, it begins to resonate with you, and then the whole universe begins to shift in your favour. The closer you resonate with what you want, the closer you get to having it. Similarly, the more positive you are about what you want, the more you resonate with it, and the closer you are to creating it.

3. *Practise makes perfect.*

The more you practise visualisation, the more detail you can add to your vision. The more detail you add, the more you resonate with what you want. You know how the rest goes.

4. *The more detailed your visualisation, the more effective it is.*

Take your time and build your vision slowly. Little by little, add more layers, gradually giving them more detail as you go. This allows your vision to become more real. It allows it to grow organically, and then your subconscious is better able to absorb your vision.

Check this out. Read it slowly and savour each word:

Imagine yourself as the healthiest person in the world, full of health and vitality.

That's a simple, basic visualisation. Maybe an image of something resembling great health popped into your mind, but probably not a very effective one. And by effective, I mean an image that created *feelings*. It is the detail you add, that produces the feelings required, that make the whole thing work.

Try this one. Read slowly. Savour each word:

It is bedtime. The world is a calm place tonight. You are in a quiet, peaceful room. You lie down in your comfortable bed. A beautiful blue-white light envelops you. Soaking into every part of you. As you close your eyes and lie there, an incredible feeling of peace comes over you. All your stress flows magically right out of you. You feel yourself smile just a little bit as you begin to feel a lightness to your body and mind. Gradually, you become aware of being surrounded by six beautiful angels who have no other purpose than to lay their hands on you to ensure your ever-increasing good health. As you drift off into a deep and peaceful sleep, you know they will be there all night long. Helping you heal, rejuvenate, and regenerate as you sleep. Imagine waking up every morning feeling grateful for their heavenly attentions all night. Feeling alive. Feeling enthusiastic.

Now that's detailed! It builds, and it grows. It escalates. It *works*. You could even improve on it by seeing the clothes they are wearing, the expression on their faces and the colour of their hair.

Let's try another example,

See yourself in the street surrounded by people who admire you.

That produces an OK image, but we want to create some positive feelings, don't we?

You approach a big, red, double door. Your feet make a soft but clear sound on the wooden floor. You are dressed in your finest and favourite clothes. Wearing all of your favourite colours. You look wonderful. You feel amazing. This is the moment you have waited your whole life for. You take a breath, and pause before the door. There is a hush from the people around you as they silence themselves in anticipation. You look around you and all your friends and relatives are all looking at you with love and admiration in their eyes. A few of them are giving you encouragement and congratulations.

You take another breath. You feel ready to claim the life you deserve. Really ready. You have paid your dues for long enough, and now you are ready. You are worthy of this. You reach down and turn the door handle. As you push on the door, you begin to hear them. You walk out onto the stage with your proud head held high. The crowd erupts into the loudest cheer you have ever heard. You can't help but smile as you see a thousand people on their feet. Cheering, clapping, whistling. All for you. Wow! A group of trumpets at the back of the room blow a fanfare. How popular are you? How wonderful do you feel? You are so special. Soak it up. You deserve it. You've earned it. You love it!

I wrote that straight off the top of my head, but it is a brilliant visualisation because it has movement, colour, sound—and feelings. It engages all the senses, and that makes it special. That makes it powerful. Really, powerful. I promise you that if you were to do nothing else but run through this one visualisation as you go to sleep every night, miracles will happen in your life—in time. But only if you stick with it long enough to embed the feelings.

5. *Build powerful, positive images.*

Your image must also be so strong that it dives down into the depths of your being and grabs hold with all its might. It must be so intense and have so much feeling and emotion attached to it that it will never, ever let go. Don't be put off because a visualisation doesn't feel powerful when you first begin this process. If something doesn't feel right, what do you do? Give up? No!

Instead, go back to number three in this list— *practise*. You have to keep building the image until your new positive image is bigger and better than your current negative one. That is how you build a powerful, positive image. Practise. Persistence. Determination. This may sound hard, but it's a lot easier than struggling to make stuff happen outside of yourself.

So do it! You will love yourself for it.

6. *Within your own imagination, you are only limited by that imagination.*

You haven't lost that extra weight yet because you can't get an image of your desired result. You are not rich yet because you can't see it in your imagination. You keep "trying" but failing to achieve things because you have not given your subconscious the proper instructions to create it for you.

Humans have accomplished many, many amazing things over the centuries. We have spent our entire existence overcoming, adapting, improvising, and creating. There are those of us who have healed great emotional pain. Others who have healed physical health problems. We have travelled to the moon and back. We will go to Mars. We will discover free energy that doesn't deplete the planet. All it takes—all anything takes—is one person to believe it is possible and have the courage to begin moving towards it. All it takes is to build a powerful enough vision of what you want *before* *y*ou do anything else.

Anything you want for yourself is limited only by your own thinking. Let your imagination run wild. Go crazy. You have everything to gain and nothing to lose. Go for it in your own head. You don't even have to tell anyone. Until they see the smile of satisfaction begin to form on your face, that is. Until they see the bounce in your step. Until they notice the changes taking place in you; the ones that are impossible to miss.

Then you can tell them, "Yes, I have an imagination, and it's amazing."

GOOD FEELINGS

As I mentioned before, changing your life has to begin with you. If you love and accept yourself as you are now, it is so much easier to create what you want. If the man is right, his world will be right. So let's begin our feast of visualisations with some powerful images designed to make you feel really good. From these powerful images of yourself, all else can grow.

As the author, Rhonda Byrne, says, "Feeling good means feeling good," but most of us just don't feel that good. Most of us feel OK. Or worse than OK. I don't know about you, but I want to feel amazing. So let's create some amazing feelings, shall we?

Begin by sitting somewhere comfortable. On your own in a quiet room is best, but if you can hear noises, that's OK, too. Just make sure you won't be disturbed. Worrying about someone walking in on you is no way to relax. Ask anyone who has ever used a public loo with no lock on the door. Talking of loos, I have often retreated to one in order to give myself a quick pick-me-up with a visualisation. It really doesn't matter where you do it. What matters is that you do it often. The more you do it, the clearer a vision becomes, and the clearer it becomes, the closer it gets to reality.

The next ten visualisations are the ones that I have recorded for you.

Visualisation no. 1: The Power Within

Close your eyes. Stay very still. Ignore the need to move. Override it and stay still. The longer you stay still, the more relaxed you become. Notice your breathing. Feel your chest moving in and out. Around the area of your heart you begin to notice a glowing light. It is a warm glow. A feeling of love and gentleness begins to come from it.

Do nothing. Just notice the light. Observe it getting warmer, brighter, clearer. What colour is it? Begin to feel the changing sensations in your body. Begin to notice that the more you accept the light, the more it grows. Notice as it begins to seep into the whole of your chest. Feel the difference as it enters your shoulders, your arms, your hands and fingers. Really feel it as its warmth travels throughout your whole torso. Now your pelvis is glowing with warmth and exhilaration. Down your legs, all the way to your feet and your toes. Your whole body is glowing now. You might be feeling a tingling all over. Maybe a little buzz of deliciousness.

Now allow the light to expand outside of you. Just a little at first. Then more. You control it. Find where it feels best. Is it expanded a foot away from you? Farther? Or just close to your body? Play with it. Enjoy it. Feel it. What does it sound like? It is alive, this light, pulsating. It is the life force within you. Allow it to begin shrinking. Let it shrink all the way back to your heart. Feel its strength, its vibration. Notice its effect on your mind, on your body.

Hold on to that feeling. Decide to keep that feeling with you for the rest of the day and night. Say thank you to the power you believe in for this amazing feeling you have. Open your eyes and just sit for a moment feeling it.

All you have to do is read through that a few times. Slow it right down. Don't rush it. Let there be a pause where there is a full stop. Allow each sentence to sink fully into your subconscious before you move on to the next. You will find that you can feel it just by reading it. But then try to do it with your eyes closed. Don't worry about getting it right. I promise it will be right for you, and that's all that matters. And the more you practise, the better you will get at it.

Now, how about creating some happiness? I think we all want to be happy, but we just keep getting lost in life, don't we? Things to do, things to pay for, family drama, work drama. We simply forget that happiness should always be our number-one priority. When we are happy—and I mean truly happy—we cope so much better with everything else. We are stronger. We are healthier. Most importantly, we attract the good things in life.

Let's say you are lonely and want romantic love in your life. How attractive are you when you are feeling sad about being alone? As I look back and remember myself as a teenager and young man, I can see that I was causing all of my own pain and loneliness. I was feeling so low that I was simply the least attractive person around for miles. If I had focused on raising my happiness level instead of on my loneliness, I would have become more attractive instantly. So don't focus on what you don't want because it just attracts more of what you don't want. Try doing this a few times a day instead.

Visualisation no. 2: Celebration Time

Close your eyes and relax. Imagine you are in your favourite place. All around you all you can see are bright colours. Celebratory fireworks are safely going off. Party poppers are flying off everywhere. Champagne bottles are being popped. The bangs and pops of them all are intermingling. The whole world seems to be celebrating you.

You soak it up. You can't help but smile. (At this point, you must force a smile even if you don't want to, and actually, why would you not want to?)Then you realise that all this isn't surrounding you at all. It is the happiness inside your own head. It is within you. It is around you. It is all there is. Bright, colourful, beautiful happiness. Pure, fantastic happiness glowing inside you. Your smile gets bigger. Your hands lift to the sky, welcoming all of this joy. (Move your hands skyward.)You have never felt so good as you do right now.

Allow all the colours and the sounds to shrink down inside you. Shrink it all the way down until all of this joy and happiness can fit into your heart. Store it there where it will be safe. Where you can feel that happiness bubbling away. Where you can remember often during your day that you have great and powerful happiness.

I included a couple of calls to action in that visualisation. It is very important that you do them. Physical action is great re-enforcement of the visualisation, but it goes even deeper than that. When you read this, your subconscious is reading, too. How could it not? It *is* you. It is the best part of you. Ninety per cent, remember? And your subconscious knows that you now know a way to feel better, to be more effective, to be healthier, whatever. If you choose *not* to do these actions, you are sending a powerful message to your subconscious. You are saying, "Don't make any effort on my part because I want to stay the same."

To that same end, I make really powerful recordings for my clients. I might be biased, but I think they are truly amazing and unique in the world today. They make such a deep and powerful connection with people that I'm told the listener can feel me touching his or her soul (actually I am). But for all that, the real power of the recordings is simply the client's choice to listen to them as often as I have explained they should. The subconscious has just listened in on that conversation. The very decision to listen, no matter what, sends a message to the subconscious that says, "I am ready to change, help me all you can."

This little book, like my recordings, hopefully will touch your soul, and these words will resonate with a deeper part of you. Your subconscious knows everything, but it needs you to show it the direction in which you want to move. That means taking action! Pick one or two of these visualisations—either one you've already read or one of the visualisations still to come—and stick with them. Do them properly for a few weeks, no matter what. Show your subconscious that you are ready to change, that you are ready to be happy. It is only imagination, after all. You don't even have to get off your couch for this, for goodness' sake.

Now, here is a visualisation that is a little more fanciful than the previous two. I guarantee that it will stick in your subconscious if done regularly.

Visualisation no. 3: Feeling Alive

Imagine you are on holiday and you have the opportunity to go out on a boat to see the dolphins. The weather is warm and sunny. You get on the boat with the other tourists. Everyone is happy and relaxed. All of you are excited to see the dolphins today. The crew of the boat all look after you very well as you chug out into the bay. You zig a little, and you zag a little. All watching, searching. Who will be the first to spot them?

Finally, someone shouts, "There they are!" As the boat moves off towards them, you get a sense of excitement and wonder. Finally, you are surrounded by the happiest, most playful creatures you have ever seen. You can't help but call to them. You are shouting and waving and smiling. The dolphins are leaping and calling back and splashing you. This is the most amazing experience you have ever had. See the blue colour of the ocean. Hear the dolphins call and splash. Feel the spray as they land on top of the water.

Now take this whole scene deep inside you. Feel those dolphins playing. Really feel their playfulness. Really experience their happiness. What does it feel like having all those dolphins swimming around in your bloodstream? What is it like to have all that happiness and playfulness occupying your immune system? Just take a moment to thank the dolphins for their company. Ask them to stay with you today as you go about your business. Open your eyes, and as you do, decide to keep the feeling of these beautiful and happy creatures within you. Now smile.

When you do this visualisation, you fill your subconscious with all of those wonderful feelings. When you do it two or three times a day your subconscious takes onboard those feelings as an instruction. That inner intelligence then recreates them throughout your day. All day long you keep remembering those feelings, and if you remember a feeling, you feel it all over again. Honestly, it is so lovely, you just have to do it.

I really think that these first visualisations are the most important. They are the foundations of a new you. It is vital that you take your time and feel really good when you do them because when you feel like that, all things become possible. I work with many different clients to address many different problems. But the one thing they all have in common is that they move on and get to where they are going a hell of a lot quicker once they begin focusing on feeling good—about themselves, and within themselves.

Believe me, I know what I'm talking about. I pushed against the tide for decades. But the only struggle I was really involved in was against myself. My life has been, in turn, tragic, pitiful, miserable, interesting, and now exciting. That was, in a nutshell, the progression of how I felt throughout my life. Guess what happened just before it became exciting?

That's right, I started to effectively visualise what I wanted. I began to create the life I wanted by seeing it first in my mind's eye. I decided to make something happen, and I kept visualising it, and I kept moving towards it, until it happened,

I would urge anyone to stop struggling against or towards anything. Simply concentrate on feeling good and everything else will come trotting along just like a faithful pony. (How's that for an image?) Keep imagining what you want, and let your subconscious take care of the rest.

Here is another visualisation for you. Really let your imagination run away with you this time. Nothing matters, it's just playtime for the mind.

Visualisation no. 4: The New You

You are strolling down the road. It is a beautiful sunny day. The weather is warm, and you are feeling good. Really good. About twenty feet in front of you there is another you. Keeping the same pace as you, they are even happier. In fact, you have never seen anyone look happier. Whilst they are outwardly calm, you—knowing you as you do—can see that there is a bounce to their step. You cannot see it, but you know there is a terrific smile on their face. Their shoulders are relaxed but square. This other you looks amazing. You begin to wish that you could feel this good.

You notice people are greeting them. Shaking hands. Patting them on the back. This is an amazing sight. Did you just see someone throw petals on the floor? Can you hear a choir singing? This is wonderful. Amazing. You decide to take a closer look. As you walk closer you begin to actually feel the positive energy that is left in their wake. It just makes you hunger for more, drawing you forward like a traction beam. You feel it getting stronger and stronger as you get right up behind them. It begins to feel as though you, too, are feeling that good. It feels like people are talking to you. Everyone wants to know you. To speak to you. To be a part of you.

At this point you step right on inside that other you, and quite naturally and peacefully, you become them. Really experience the pleasure of feeling this good. Notice the changing sensations in your body. The slight tingling of your skin. The smile in your eyes. The bounce of your step. You notice a bench. Take a seat and just breath in the air of your new and beautiful world. You are, indeed, everything you ever wanted to be. Congratulate yourself. Feel a great love for yourself. Take a moment to sit with these feelings and then open your eyes, and choose to keep the feelings with you for the rest of the day.

Loving and accepting ourselves is the single most important thing we can do. If you want to change your life, change what you think of yourself and what you feel about yourself. I struggled to become "successful" for decades, but I simultaneously hated myself for *not* being "successful." My progress was so slow a snail could have done it faster. It was only when I stopped hating myself for who I was, and began using my powerful imagination to visualise what I wanted, that the light finally went on.

If you pull your attention away from whatever makes you dislike yourself, your switch will get flicked on, too. Nothing will make a bigger impact on you. Concentrate all your attention on who you want to be; and how you want to feel. Everything else will take care of itself, I promise.

Visualisation no. 5: Love Yourself

As you sit quietly, become aware of the very centre of your being. Where is it? Where is the centre of your own universe within you? As you focus all of your attention there, become aware of a tiny, tiny sparkle of light. Watch it twinkle. Notice that it looks just like a distant bright star in the night sky. Continue to observe your very own brightly twinkling star as I remind you what a star is.

Our sun is a star. The stars are the powerhouse of creation. They are the driving force of the universe. If the universe were battery powered, then the stars would be the batteries. They give light and warmth. They are the gravity that planets cling to, the glue that holds it all together. Our sun is one of the smallest stars. There are suns out there a hundred times bigger. They are huge, beautiful, loving sources of immense power. And you have a tiny one of them twinkling deep inside yourself right now. Imagine all that energy glowing inside you.

Imagine the love that glows from it seeping into every cell and molecule of you. Feel the glow of it reaching all parts of you. All the way from the tip of your toes to the top of your head. Bask in this glow. Accept this love. Accept its healing power. Accept that you are a star. You are everything that a star is. You have power. You have light. You have great warmth. You have gravity, pulling towards you all that you desire. Really sit with this for a while. Just feel it. When you are ready, open your eye. Just stay there and feel it. As you go through your day, keep remembering that star twinkling in the heart of you. Every time you do, give yourself a little smile of satisfaction.

Now, remember, the power of visualisation is in repetition. Practise it morning, noon, and night. Use whichever visualisation feels good to you. Do what feels right and you will never get it wrong. It doesn't have to be exactly like mine, either. These are just ideas that come to me as I write or speak. Maybe I channel them, I don't know, but I have been doing this stuff ad lib for over a decade. I just start and the words come. I believe they are very powerful *because* I don't think about them. They go directly from my subconscious to yours. So just use them as a starting point. Then allow your own ideas to flow from your own powerful imagination, and they will be as powerful as mine.

USING VISUALISATION FOR SPECIFIC PURPOSES

Now that we have covered the basics of building good feelings, let's look at some specific examples of powerful visions for some of the most common challenges. Even if any of these are not a current challenge for you, read about it anyway. There are little gems of inspiration within them all.

Giving up smoking

Two things instantly spring to mind here. Firstly, if you are *trying* to give up smoking, your subconscious will take that as an instruction and ensure that is all you do—try. You must make the decision that it is done. Now. In your own mind you have to have decided enough is enough. Secondly, don't ever focus on what you don't want. *Always* focus on what you do want. It's not giving up smoking; it's becoming a non-smoker.

I struggled with smoking from a very early age. I started inhaling when I was twelve and hated it by the time I was fifteen. After many years of trying to stop, I was eventually well over thirty by the time I decided to actually do it. This was when I inadvertently created Five Times. I started doing the affirmation "I am a non-smoker," all day every day. After about a week, I put a date in the diary to stop in about three weeks' time. When the date came round, I was ready to just leave it all behind. After I stopped, I kept on with Five Times for another month or so, and gradually I didn't need it anymore.

Five Times works! Use it for anything you want to achieve. Make it the first step in whatever you decide to do.

Try this visualisation. Take your time and savour the words. Remember that it's all about the feelings, so pay attention to what's happening inside you as you go.

Visualisation no. 6: The Pile of Vile!

You are sitting on top of every packet of cigarettes you have ever bought. How high off the ground are you? What does the pile look like? How do you feel knowing what all these cigarettes have cost you? As you sit there, you see all your family and friends surrounding you. They look sad, and you begin to wonder why.

You gradually realise that you are actually tied to a stake coming up through your pile of cigarettes. It is Guy Fawkes Night*. You are the Guy, and below you is your Pile of Vile. The realisation hits you at the deepest level: cigarettes are your downfall, your destruction, your end. A lone man steps forward to the bottom of the pile. He is not here to save you but to light you up one last time.

As the flames begin to take hold, you realise that the only person who can save you is you. It is time to make a choice. Just as it gets too hot to bear, you realise that your bonds are broken and you are free to choose; and you choose to walk away from these things forever!

You walk away into a bright, healthy future surrounded by your loved ones who now get to keep you for so much longer. Everybody is cheering and clapping. The trumpets are playing, and the fireworks are going off. You realise they are no longer celebrating Guy Fawkes but celebrating you. You turn around to see the blazing fire in the distance firmly behind you. No Guy, just a Pile of Vile burning up. Now harmless and without any draw for you at all. Move forward to a wonderful future.

* Guy Fawkes tried (and failed) to blow up the English parliament on 5 November,1605. Guy Fawkes Night is celebrated annually across the UK with fires and fireworks.

As always, I made that visualisation up as I wrote this book. Apart from editing it for spelling and punctuation, no changes have been made. I have never had that idea before, despite helping more people with smoking than I can count. It is absolutely jam-packed with messages that the subconscious will act on. If you listen to the MP3 version once or twice a day, it will help you immensely in becoming a non-smoker.

Weight loss

Obesity is one of the world's biggest problems. We have so many issues with weight and food, and so many people make themselves miserable with it. But as usual, if you can't see what you want because of the fog of what you *don't* want, you are destined never to change.

This is the one case where I don't tell people to build a bigger vision of themselves. In this case, you need a smaller vision of yourself, to be sure.

Visualisation no. 7: Good Food Alley!

See yourself walking along a wide, beautiful boulevard. The sun is shining, and you are feeling really good. As you walk along, you see food stands appearing on each side of the path. On one side, all the food is rubbish stuff—unhealthy and bad for you. This food blocks your arteries, saps your energy, makes you fat, robs you of a fun and active lifestyle. It drains your energy just looking at it. On the other side, where the sun seems to shine brighter, is all the good food. The food that feeds your mind and body with nutrition. That gives you energy, vitality, good health, a long and active life. It uplifts you just to look at it.

Imagine you have the power to obliterate anything you choose to. What is your weapon of choice? Take it out now and begin firing on the side of the walk with all the rubbish food. Blow it away. Keep firing until you have destroyed everything. Leave nothing but burning wreckage.

Smile with a sense of great satisfaction. Discard your weapon and step over to the good food, and as you stroll the length of it all, begin to feel inspired about new meals you can cook and new foods to eat. As you stroll down, you feel lighter and more focused than you have in a long time. Life is feeling good again. You are feeling good again.

As you arrive at the end of the row, see yourself at your perfect weight. What are you wearing? How do you stand? What do you sound like? What are you saying to your friends? What are they saying to you? Step right on into this new you. Feel this now. Walk on down the street feeling lighter than air. Every happy step you take makes you feel lighter and lighter. Take a breath and decide to keep these new feelings with you.

There are two important points to remember here. Firstly, it is essential that you keep working on these visions. Let them grow. Let them develop. Let them become a part of you. If you are a long way from your perfect self, it takes time to close the gap, both emotionally and in terms of actually losing the weight. So the second point is that if you have a very long way to go, focus on the next milestone and build a vision for that. Don't get depressed because the top of the mountain is so high. That will stop you from even getting out of the foothills. Set intermediate goals: base camp, acclimatisation climbs, and finally, the summit bid.

The end of each visualisation should always be for you to get an image of yourself having reached the next step, whatever that is for you. Make life easier for yourself. Build that vision of the next step and stop at nothing until you get there. Just get focused on the next half a stone. You will arrive at each of these smaller goals as quick as a flash. Then you can more easily move on to the next.

Having more money

Oh, money, glorious money. I can write a book about how *not* to have enough money. I'm going to do you a huge favour and not bore you with the details of my earlier life of poverty and struggle, but what I will say is this: without a vision of yourself having money, you will never have it. It is the same story throughout the whole of this book. Unless you can see and feel it first, you can never have it. Ever!

Once I discovered there was such a thing as a positive attitude, I set out to make money. Now, at last, twenty-six years after that fateful day, having learnt many lessons and now doing things right, I can finally look back and see the utter futility of virtually every stressful, painful, frustrating, heartbreaking day of that quarter of a century. The sheer desperation to be "successful" was excruciating. If there was a brick wall, I would bang my head against it. If there was a hamster wheel, I would fight for my right to jump on. If there was a way to work my arse off for too little money, I was there with my hand up.

I can now tell you for sure that you need to feel successful, even when you are in the gutter. You need to feel rich, even when you are poor. You need to know in your heart of hearts that you can climb out of that pit and live a better life, and you need to be prepared to do whatever it takes. Even if all you can do—for now—is to build a bigger vision for yourself.

I can honestly admit that my big block to making money was my shame at not having any. Think about that. How stupid can you get? That shame paralysed me. Totally and utterly paralysed me. It stopped me from feeling good about myself. It blocked my creativity. It stopped me from recognising my true worth. It blinded me to my talents and gifts. Every time I thought of something wonderful to give to the world, it shouted in my ear, "You can't do that! You're not good enough!" This was the overriding feeling that inhabited my whole being for so much of my life. Whenever I wanted anything good, that was what I heard and felt at the deepest level. It was learning to visualise effectively that finally rid me of that demon.

Shame is so debilitating. If you have no money and are struggling to pay your bills, hold your head up high. Be proud of who you are. Be proud that you are reading this book and learning how to change your life. If you have that voice in you that I used to have, use Five Times to shout louder and drown that negative voice out of you.

Stand up and tell the world that *you* are changing your situation, once and for all. Many of us have done it before you, and many will do it after you. You should be one of us. You can be one of us. You are one of us.

But you need a powerful vision of your next step, whatever that is. If you have a large bill to pay, that's the thing you need to have a vision about. Don't allow real life to distract you. Just visualise paying that bill so it can manifest in the now. Retreat into your imagination and feel yourself walking into the bank, getting out your money, saying hello to the cashier, and paying the bill with a sense of pride, joy, and satisfaction.

If your next step is taking your business to the next level, what does that mean? More money? More customers? What are you going to offer them? Just imagine the sparks of creativity lighting up your whole company, or you running round the office shouting, "I've had a great idea!" Pick one thing and feel it often. Prove to your subconscious that you want it. It will do the rest.

But don't forget you need a bigger vision too. You might find it useful to think of it in terms of years. A bigger vision is where you will be in a few years' time; or even ten years' time. The next step is probably next week or next month. A bigger vision gives your whole life a bigger purpose. It is a guiding light for all your decisions and choices you make each day. "Am I moving towards my goals, or away from them?"

Wanting to be "rich", however, is nowhere near good enough. You have to have some idea of what you will offer for the money you want. You need to be specific about what success means to you. My problem for all those years was that my definition of success was just too big and uncompromising. I just didn't recognise any of the stepping stone successes that I could have built on. I always thought I was failing because I had such a bad definition of success.

Every time I managed to pay a bill, I just went straight into worrying about the next one. You have to celebrate every tiny, little victory. *Everything* should be celebrated. That's where success and wealth come from. So start celebrating your bills and the money you manage to pay them with.

Don't be ashamed of where you are. I know I have just said this, but it is worth stating again, I think. Nothing will hold you down more effectively than feeling ashamed for being broke. Most successful people will be able to tell you funny stories about when they had nothing. So many of us have been there. The only thing to be ashamed of is if you accept that as your reality. Just because you are broke, fat, lonely, a smoker, or unsuccessful today doesn't mean you are going to be the same way tomorrow.

The next visualisation will help you create a money mindset. I've aimed it at the lowest level, which I like to call . . .

In the shit!

I lived at this level for more than two decades. Constantly worrying. Never having enough to make ends meet. Bouncing cheques. Robbing Peter to pay Paul. Constantly borrowing more and more from a bank that was doing their best to take me ever deeper into debt. That same bank charging me twenty-five pounds every time I bounced a cheque, making my situation even worse. It was a harrowing experience and completely draining.

I want you to know that if you are at this level now, there is a way out. In fact, there are thousands of ways out. Your subconscious can choose from all of them and guide you through the maze of possibilities. But it has to be shown what you want first. You have to give it your instructions. You have to change how you *feel* about your situation and about money in general.

Up next is the most important piece of information I can give you, and the most vital for you to understand if you want to change anything in your life.

You don't have to change your feelings every minute of every day.

Just start, twice or thrice a day, visualising what you want instead. Practise building that one powerful vision over and over again. This is a new reference point for your imagination, a new focus for your subconscious mind to lock onto, a brand-new guidance system for your on-board computer. Those new good feelings will begin seeping into every aspect of your day, gradually smoothing the waters, and little by little, lifting the corners of your mouth.

Visualisation no. 8: My Bills Are Paid

You are sitting in a beautiful, clean, white, comfortable room. You are alone and feeling calm, peaceful, and contented. The sun is shining in through the open windows, and the weather is warm. On the coffee table in front of you are all your current bills laid out neatly, and in order of importance. As you look at them you have a feeling of control and excited anticipation. Today is a new kind of day. Remember the old days when you used to worry about your bills. That seems so far away now. On the table is also a beautiful, box containing your writing materials. Open the lid and take out your favourite pen. Lean forward and put a great big tick on every one of your bills. Take your time and savour the sensation of knowing each tick is another one paid.

When they all have a big tick on them, pick up your paid-bills folder and very neatly, and with great reverence, file away your paid bills into the folder for your records. Sit back when the work is done, and begin to plan what to spend your spare money on now that there are no more bills to pay.

Think about a holiday, a new car, new furniture—all the things that disposable income can buy. Relax in the knowledge that you can have so much more nowadays. As you are thinking of all the wonderful things you can have, a noise from the open doorway distracts you, and as you glance over, you see paper money blowing into your house on a summer breeze. Loads and loads of lovely money pouring into your beautiful home, your beautiful life. You laugh and laugh at the wonder of it all. You begin to feel very blessed.

That visualisation, done properly and frequently, is enough to begin turning the tide for you. Create the feelings and your subconscious finds ways to produce more of those feelings for you. But you need to show it the way. Show it what you want by sitting with that visualisation at least twice a day. You *can* do this.

I also want to share with you two powerful aids to financial—or any—success:

Gratitude. Avoid feeling sorry for yourself. This is the biggest enemy of getting what we want. Feeling sorry for ourselves is just visualising what we don't want. It is a nasty little habit that keeps us stuck. Look for things to be grateful for. Gratitude is one of the most powerful tools we have for creating good in our lives. There really is so much to be grateful for. Drag yourself away from self-pity and write out twenty things you appreciate. Take your time, really get the feelings. As you write, you are visualising, so do it well. Do it daily. The really magical results will begin showing up when you can find things to appreciate hidden in the 'bad' stuff that is going on in your life.

Do it like this:

Thank you for my lovely wife.

Thank you for the amazing food I ate last night.

Thank you for my money.

Thank you for the great news.

Thank you for my good friends.

Thank you for my wonderful holiday.

Thank you for the lessons I am learning.

Thank you for helping me deal with difficult people.

Thank you for my joy.

Thank you for my happiness.

Mix it up, one after another. Some are things you have and some are things you want. Just jumble them all up. See how many you can come up with at a time. I do this as I fall asleep and again when I wake up. You will feel your whole body relax and soften as you do this; as you allow the good feelings to become part of you; as you invite them in with the words you speak. Do this often. Treat it as a ritual. Remind yourself of all that you have to be grateful for.

You only have to watch the news, or look online anywhere, anytime to find less fortunate people than yourself who still manage to have a grateful smile on their face. There are people who have no food, no home, no security, no arms, no legs. You have nothing to be ungrateful for, believe me.

Celebration. Look for *any* reason to celebrate. It doesn't matter how foolish or little it seems, celebrate it. Create the winning habit of celebration. Remember, it's all about showing the subconscious what you want. If you are broke and you manage to pay a bill, that is reason enough to celebrate. It doesn't have to mean great big, expensive celebrations. It can be a cupcake with a candle, coffee with a good friend, leaving work an hour early, anything. Personally I like to jump up and punch the air with a great big whoop of delight. It's simple, easy, and is a whole body experience. It's great programming for my subconscious.

I won a huge three litre bottle of lager in a raffle. Eventually, after a few months we had a birthday party where enough people were gathered to warrant opening it. We always thought that when it was finally emptied we would fill it with our coins. But, surprisingly, the bottle neck is so small the only coin that fits through it is a five pence. At first I was disappointed, but very quickly I realised that I probably would never spend another five pence coin again. Now I can't wait to get my hands on them so I can put them in my bottle. Now I celebrate every one of those little silver gems that crosses my palm!

There is always *something* to celebrate. It just depends on how you choose to look at things. Every time I get a five pence in my pocket now, I feel like I've hit the jackpot. Find things to celebrate. Find a way to do it that suits you, and as long as you mark it in a way that the subconscious can understand that it is a celebration. Then your job is done, and you can watch the magic begin to happen. Work at this until your whole life begins to feel like a celebration.

Both of these habits, gratitude and celebration, go hand in hand and create the most amazing good feelings. Make them rituals in your life by focusing on them daily.

Good feelings attract good things!

Practise these things until they become habit. Practise them until they become real. Act *as if*, and it soon will be.

Health

As I mentioned earlier, I specialised in stress management for most of the time I was a practising hypnotherapist. I found that no matter what the client's presenting problem, if we could get rid of the stress, half the problem would get up and walk away by itself. Stress is the poison that destroys the mind, body, and soul of a person. As far as illness is concerned, if stress didn't cause it, it certainly makes it worse.

So how do you know if you are stressed? Easy! If you are not a Buddhist monk, you are probably stressed. If you work at a job you hate, if you want something and it pains you not to have it, if you are frustrated, worried, angry, impatient, tearful, or if you think your life is not perfect, you are stressed to some extent or other.

I can guarantee you that if you moan a lot, you're stressed. And surprise, surprise—that stress is actually caused, in a large part, by your moaning. The paradox of stress is this: everybody thinks when those external problems go away they will be stress free. But actually the reverse is true. When we focus on lowering our stress levels, then those external problems go away all by themselves. For the same reasons we have already talked about; focus on the inside, not on the outside.

Lowering our stress levels increases our connection to the subconscious, so we are more creative, intuitive, inspired. We see things coming so prevent the bad things from occurring in the first place by making better choices, and if we need to, we cope with things better when they do happen.

But let's get back to the physical. The mind and body function best when they are calm and relaxed. The energy flows freely, as does the blood, the digestive system, and everything else inside you. Block this flow with the tension of stress and the body will suffer. There are many causes of illness, and many emotional and psychological blocks to healing, but removing stress is the most important first step to health and vitality.

Relieving stress is so important that my *Stress-Buster Elite!* Is now the only remaining scripted recording I produce. Because the script for the recording (not one of mine) is so damn good I could never improve it. It is twenty minutes long, and if listened to at the both ends of the working day for four weeks, it can transform a person so greatly that they hardly recognise who they used to be. I'm talking about people who were having seven or eight panic attacks a day, people who were so stressed they couldn't even fill out my consultation form.

My point here is that no matter how stressed you are, never believe that you have to stay that way. I have proved hundreds of times that, even the worse stress can be completely eradicated in as little as one month.

If you want to be healthy, get rid of your stress first. Eat right and get plenty of exercise, then build a powerful vision of a healthy you, full of vitality and a love for life.

Visualisation no. 9: Healthy me!

You are sitting comfortably in a beautiful, clean, sunny room. The temperature is comfortable, and you are dressed to relax. You are smiling because you feel so good about the world right now. Across the room from you, on the wall, is a picture that is a life-size image of your perfect self. This person is smiling back at you, and whenever you look at the picture, you can actually feel the love coming from the you in the picture to the you in the room.

As you gaze into the loving eyes of this perfect you, a feeling of calm flows through your entire blood stream. Your immune system begins to actually glow with the sheer pleasure of being here with the perfect you. Every molecule in your body begins to do a little Irish jig. As you now stand up, your whole amazing mind and body is vibrating to a higher, healthier degree.

Walk across the room and as you reach the picture on the wall, your perfect self reaches out a hand to you, inviting you to step up. You take the hand and step into your higher self. You become your perfect self. Look down now where the old you was sitting and feel the surge of power within you now that you are perfectly healthy. Feel the vitality, the energy, the life force surging around and through you.

Now as the perfect you, step back down and sit down again. As you glance over to the picture notice the Old You is in the picture and recognise that you are now the perfect you. Healthy. Full of vitality. Loving life.

A few points to remember about this visualisation:

Like all visualisation, doing it once or twice will achieve nothing. Doing it twice or thrice every day, however, will affect you at the deepest level. I'm not saying this is all you need to be healthy, but it's a great place to start.

While you should start with this visualisation, be sure to allow yours to morph into something that belongs to you and you alone. Make it yours. Make it resonate. Make it *real*!

You should stretch these visualisations to at least five minutes. I have written this, and the other visualisations quickly to show you the kind of thing you should be doing, but in reality, the feelings take a while longer to create than the time it takes just to read that visualisation. You have to do it until you feel it. When you start to feel it, start the clock. No feelings, no results! Do this for all your visualising.

Finding love

From the very first time I saw a girl I liked, girls just wanted to be my friend. I suffered rejection after rejection. My self-esteem, by the time I was in my early twenty's, was broken, shattered, and completely battered.

But one day, a long time later, I woke up to the fact that it was all my own doing. What had paralyzed me—and made me so unattractive—were my own negative feelings about myself. I genuinely felt as though I was unwanted, unlovable, and unworthy. The vision I held of myself was one of constant rejection. So, of course, that is what I got. Over and over and over again. Until I saw the light.

I can promise you that if you are feeling lonely, there is only one person creating these feelings within you. Only one person causing your pain, and only one person who can turn it around. It doesn't have to go on forever. It doesn't even have to be the same tomorrow. Remember, all it takes is a decision.

I have now been happily married, at the time of writing this book, for eight years. I am a gorgeous, fabulous man. I am great fun. I am lovely. I am lovable. I am attractive. I still look the same, but I am a totally different person now than the one I just described to you. I like myself, I really do. I'm a nice guy, and I have a huge amount to give to the world.

It took a lot of effort to have this kind of relationship with myself. If you want a good relationship with another person, you need to have a good relationship with yourself first. Go back to some of those earlier visualisations. Get started on building yourself up from the inside out. Then give this visualisation a go.

Visualisation no.10: Spring Clean!

Take a moment to pause as you sit comfortably. As you begin to relax and sink deeper into the chair, things begin to become clearer for you. They become so clear, in fact, that you find yourself looking into your own mind. As you start to poke around this vast cavern, you come across some funny memories of happy days.

You can take some out of the boxes or cupboards and have a closer look at them. Who is there? What are you wearing? How old are you?

Now, have a stroll around and see what you can find that makes you feel alone. What are the thoughts and feelings buried away in here that make you feel so low ? Get your vacuum cleaner out and start cleaning up the house. Anything you don't like can be sucked right up out of it. Turn on your favourite music. Turn the volume up. How does it feel to be spring-cleaning your mind?

Turn it into a party—a celebration of a new you. Really go to town. Get in all the corners. Clean out all the shelves, the cupboards, the chests. Look under everything to make sure no bad thoughts about yourself or your loneliness are left behind. Feel the pleasure it gives you cleaning this stuff out.

Now, finally, sit down on a nice comfy sofa and look at how clean and bright it looks in here. Imagine now that powerful positive words begin floating in. You can see them flowing around the room, resting on the walls and the floor and the ceiling. Wonderful words of love and joy and happiness, relationships, fun, company, companionship. Feel some of them getting bigger, brighter. Some of them shout at you whilst others whisper.

Wrap yourself up in them. Allow them to become a part of you. Soak them up. Soak them into every molecule. Now taking those new, wonderful feelings with you, step back out of your mind and see yourself walking down the street still wrapped up in glorious new feelings. What do you feel like? What do you look like? What is your life like now you are this happy?

Bring these magical feelings back with you as you open your eyes.

Problems

Whether they are big or small, our lives will be dogged with problems. But every problem carries a thousand different solutions—as well as opportunities. The Chinese even use the same word for problem and opportunity! Your subconscious can sift through all the possibilities and find the perfect one for you, but only if you show it what you want by building a powerful vision. Problem or opportunity? How you look at it, or how you feel about it, defines how your subconscious will deal with it.

Visualisation no.11: Solutions!

You are alone in your perfect house. You are safe and surrounded by all of your favourite things. Take a moment to move through your house and experience all the lovely things you own. Feel the floor beneath you. Feel your clothes against your skin. Feel the pleasure all your stuff gives you. As you move through the house, you become aware that you feel calm and peaceful. You sit in a beautiful chair and relax as you take a deep breath.

You sit there comfortably, thinking about the newfound trust and faith that has grown in you in recent times. This faith and trust has solved your problems and produced many rich solutions. It has brought you to this house and all these beautiful things. It can bring you anything you desire—health, wealth, peace of mind. All there for you to pick off the shelf whenever you choose to focus on them.

Many times a big step towards any of your desires is a solution to a problem. As you sit there, you realise that problems are our friends. They provide opportunities for us to shine, to excel, and to grow. Solving them is satisfying. Solving problems is how we get ahead. The more we recognise this power within us, the more we can actually look forward to the problems that come our way.

Sit comfortably and contemplate these things. Feel the solutions to everything surrounding you, floating around the room, touching the walls, the floor, the ceiling. Reach out and grab one. Is it right for your situation? If it isn't, let it go with grace, knowing the next one might be.

Just sit and peacefully sift through the thousands of possible solutions. Take your time, enjoy the process.

When you are ready, open your eyes and continue with your day.

OK, the important thing here is this: the solution probably won't come to you while you do this visualisation. The visualisation is to show your subconscious what you want and that you trust it to give it you. You must finish the visualisation with feelings of trust and faith that the answer is coming.

For me, it is always the middle of the night when I wake up with all sorts of ideas and solutions flooding my mind. For you, it might be on the golf course, while you are swimming, walking, climbing, driving. It will almost certainly be when you are *not* thinking of the problem. Remember, your conscious mind cannot solve your problems, so you actually block the solution coming from your subconscious mind by struggling with it in your conscious mind.

Imagine the solution has already happened and the problem is way behind you. Don't worry. It soon will be for real.

Success

Whatever it is you want to achieve, you have to picture the end result. You have to practise it until you get it. Otherwise, you won't recognise it when it comes along, will you? Once you have chosen what that end result will be, write it down, speak it as an affirmation, draw pictures of it, make a vision board. Do everything you can to embed it in your entire being. The more you do to show your subconscious that this is what you want, the more likely your goal will come to fruition.

Once your end result is embedded in your subconscious, the most amazing things will begin to happen. You will be driven by inspired action. You will move from confusion and self-doubt to self-assuredness and certainty. You will be given creative solutions. You will feel effortlessly motivated. You will truly begin to enjoy life. Everything will become easier. Whatever it is you want, you have the power to make it happen—on the inside first.

Success is something you have to entice. By constantly returning to what you want in your own imagination, you are proving yourself deserving. All the obstacles you face are tests. If success thinks you don't want her badly enough, she will walk away from you in the other direction.

A long time ago, I read a book by a lady healer. She had been in a car accident that left her with a damaged brain. She set out on a healing journey that lasted nine years. (Apparently the brain takes a long time to heal) At one point she was awarded a huge financial payout from the other driver's insurance company. She was awarded hundreds of thousands of pounds. I'm afraid I don't recall the exact amount, nor the lady's name, but what I do recall is the fact that she gave every penny to charity and never touched any of it.

She was not going to benefit in any way from her injury because of the subconscious *implication* of that action. Do you think she was going to let anything get in the way of what she wanted? Not on your life! She made sure her subconscious knew exactly what her chosen outcome was—no matter what!

Your subconscious responds to the implication of your actions—or non-actions—even more powerfully than your visualisations. This is why I keep banging on about proving it to your subconscious. Everything you think, say, or do is a powerful implicated instruction to your subconscious that will affect all of your tomorrows.

So consider carefully: what will the implication of your actions be today?

Visualisation no. 12: I'm A Success!

Imagine you live in another dimension. Nothing is different in this other world. Everything is just the same. Except you are different. You feel different. You think differently. You are different. In this separate reality you wake up every morning and you don't even have to look for anything to be grateful for because you are grateful that you woke up at all! You are so aware that some people didn't make it through the night.

Waking up in itself is a miracle to be grateful for, you can count it as a success! Your first success of the day, and you haven't even got out of bed yet. "Number One!" you say to yourself. As you take stock of your day ahead you can bring your focus now to your body, and focus on all the parts of you that work in harmony together creating your life on a daily basis.

Where would you be without all of this biology and chemistry working together in this way. Every time you lift a cup is nothing short of a miracle. YOU are a miracle! You are a success - all day every day, and in this new dimension you are able to recognise ALL of your successes. You are able to celebrate them, and build on them, and be grateful for them.

Imagine now that this new dimension is actually in the here and now. Spare a moment to think back to yesterday. Count out the successes you had yesterday. Every little thing you overcome is a success. When you find something you were looking for. When you have a conversation that makes you smile. When you negotiate the traffic to get to work. When you wake up breathing in the morning. When you find a coin on the floor. When you walk in the door to your home and appreciate the roof over your head. When you pay a bill, have a meal.

Smile now as you realise and recognise how lucky you are in so many ways. Realise now that success is only a matter of perspective. Choose to look for your successes today—and to count them, because surely the more successes you count, the more you attract!

Imagine now that you are standing safely in the middle of a fast moving river—except the river isn't a river of water, rather it's a flow of all good things! From your position in the centre of the flow, you are able to reach out and easily grab anything you want from life as it flows through your sphere of influence.

Take a moment now to reach out and collect all the good things you want. Grab hold of all the things that make you feel successful. As you hold on to those things, your subconscious holds on to the feelings of success to bring back with you now and forever. Take your time over this as you pick out everything you desire. All the tangible and intangible things that make you successful right now.

Give yourself a smile and carry on with your day the successful way.

CREATING HAPPINESS

Happiness is the be all and end all of everything. Without it, what are we? Everything we desire, we want because we think we will be happy when we get it. So why not focus on creating happiness in the first place? Cut out the middleman. Let the all-powerful subconscious choose the way. After all, it knows us better than we know ourselves. It knows what we want. It knows our deepest desires, and it knows the best way to bring them into being, too.

So here it is, my step-by-step guide to creating and increasing your happiness. You might find it simplistic. But I love simplicity! I have spent my whole life looking for the shortest and easiest route to achieving stuff. It is simplistic; because life is as simple as you choose to make it. Don't allow its simplicity to stop you doing it though.

Decide to be happy

Decide you are going to increase your happiness every day. Decide that nothing will stop you from blowing your happiness level through the roof. Today, and every day, you have to choose happiness over all else.

Make happiness your primary goal and all your other goals will be reached in a happy way.

You may not have all that you want right now, but choose to be happy anyway. You might be having difficulties with your children, your spouse, your teacher, your boss, the whole world. But you have the power to choose. You have the gift of decision. Choose to be happy no matter what. As Abraham Lincoln once said, "A man is as happy as he makes up his mind to be."

So step one, then, is for you to decide that your own happiness is the single most important thing there is. For now, you don't need to change anything. You just need to decide that wherever you are, whatever you have or don't have, whatever you have to deal with throughout each day, you are going to be happy.

The best summer I have ever had was the year that I decided to be great company—no matter what. It took some effort on my part to remember to think in those terms. But was it worth it? You bet it was!

Never underestimate the power of decision.

Build a vision of your happiness

Get a bottle of wine, a great big note pad, and your favourite pen, and let's begin to build a vision of your happiness.

Who do you know that always seems to be happy? This could be a friend, a relative, a pop star, a film star, anyone! Pick the person who you think is the happiest person you know. Get a picture of them looking at their happiest. Frame it. Hang it where you can see it, feel it, breathe it in.

Now list everything about them that shows you they are happy. What do they look like? What is the expression on their face? What do their eyes look like? How do they stand? How do they hold themselves? Scan the picture from top to bottom and list everything you notice. When you have finished, go over it again to see if you have missed anything. List their behaviours, their mannerisms, everything that shows how genuinely happy they are.

Next draw a picture of your percentage scale. Take your time, make it special, make it colourful. Mark (honestly) your happiness percentage. Then mark your model's percentage, too. Then do this visualisation.

Visualisation no.13: Happiness!

Now imagine you are in a theatre. On the stage in front of you is the person whose happiness level you most admire. Just being in front of them begins to make you tingle. You are smiling and enjoying them. Notice all those mannerisms you listed earlier. Notice the sparkle in their eyes, their posture, how they move, how they speak, how they breath.

Focus completely on them. Soak them up. Imagine you are moving up alongside them, standing next to them, and magically, the two of you just blending together. You become them. You are still you, but you have taken on board their aura. Their very essence of happiness has become yours.

Next to you on the stage is a giant image of your percentage scale. As you look at it and feel your own happiness and newfound pride in yourself, the percentage begins to move. Your own marker begins moving all the way up to theirs. You are equal. You are, at last, truly, deeply happy.

Carry this happiness out to the street. Greet people as you walk. Hear comments as you pass people saying, "Wow! Look how happy they are."Notice in your peripherals how people are looking at you with admiration and envy. Everybody wishes they were as happy as you.

Decide to keep these feelings and this percentage level.

Practise this every day for about five minutes at a time, and you will amaze yourself, as well as everyone who knows you.

Build a powerful image of what you want

To do this, answer these questions:

What do you want? Not what you *don't* want. What *do* you want? Be specific. If you want success, what kind of success? In what area of your life? Be precise. If you want to lose weight, how much do you want to finally weigh? What's your perfect weight? If you want money, how much exactly? Do you want to pay your bills? Or have a successful, profitable business?

Take your time with this and write it out. Make a list of positive affirmations. Write them out again and again until they look and sound exciting. Make sure you write them out in short, sweet sentences. Write them in the present tense.

Collate between five and ten positive affirmations based around your new vision for yourself. Write them out neatly on a beautiful piece of card. These now form the basis of your visualisation practise.

Now you need to ask yourself a pretty serious question:

How bad do you want it? Not bad in the sense that you feel pain for not having it yet, but bad in the sense that you are going to make a commitment to yourself and your vision. A massive, huge, unshakable commitment.

I can assure you that nothing else will do. Nothing short of this will bring it into being.

This is the pivotal point of your life. Right here, right now. Many, many people *say* they want their lives to change, but very few choose to make that commitment to themselves and their dreams. I am offering you everything you want. I am giving you the easiest, simplest, laziest way to make it happen for yourself. Transforming your life will never be easier than it is in this moment. Are you ready? Have you had enough of mediocrity yet? Are you ready to step forward and claim the life you deserve? The life you were born to live?

When you commit to do what comes next between five, or even, ten times a day, your subconscious begins to feel as though you are already there. Your imagination and your subconscious are so immensely powerful that they can make the Universe rearrange itself and bend to your will.

When you visualise what you want so often that you begin to feel it in your heart and soul as if it is real, your subconscious will make many things happen:

It creates positive behaviours that match your desire.

It produces amazing feelings that match your desire.

It feeds you insightful creativity that matches your desire.

It attracts people and circumstances that match your desire.

It replaces fear with inspiration.

It gives you the impulse to take inspired action—action that you *want* to take!

In short, it makes it happen!

So, will you do it?

Do it!

Find or build a space for creation. Return to the same spot as often as you can during the day. Take your time. Read your affirmations. Soak them up. Read them through slowly a few times. Begin to feel them. Then quietly close your eyes and allow your imagination to picture what you want.

Every time you do this, begin in the same place in the same way. Build your vision. Add colour, movement, and sound. Make it fanciful. Turn up the brightness and the volume. Make it life-size. Make it a beautiful perfect vision of the you that you want to be, that you *choose* to be.

Hold your vision for five minutes at a time until you feel it as though it is as real as can be. Sit there with it. Imagine yourself in different scenarios, with different people, but always as the New You.

The only enemy to this process is for you to rush it, so take your time.

Get the feelings!

It's always about the feelings. You have the power to create the feelings you want. That means you have the power to create anything. There is nothing more important than this gift to yourself. Do the same vision all the time so that it can grow and become more intense. If you keep swapping and changing what you are visualising (what you want) you will always be starting at the beginning again.

Anything that tries to drag you away from this all-important process is merely *resistance*.

Resistance

Taking the time out to practise the art of creation has to be our number-one priority. These moments of beautiful calm and creation are what connect us to the source of all that we can be and all that we desire. Anything that tries to pull us away from this commitment, at any time, is resistance.

Remember what I said about the Old You and the New You? Resistance is the old part of us that wants to stay the same. Beware of the lag—the time difference between your visualisations and their manifestation in the real world. You must visualise *until* it happens. You must stay the course. You must trust the process. For as long as it takes.

Don't let the Old You hold you!

Stay focused on the New You and the New You *has* to win out. It's inevitable.

Watch out for the following signs of resistance to the change:

- Thinking you don't have time for your visualisation practise. In my experience, this has proven to be the number one excuse for not visualising, therefore the number one excuse for not changing anything. Make the time. Steal the time. Enjoy the time—every time!

- That part of you that tells you that it's not working? That's the Old You that wants to stay in the comfort zone of where you are. Tell it to go away! Carry on visualising so that the subconscious knows what you really want. You must keep visualising until your subconscious believes it is real. Then and only then will it begin creating it for you. Keep at it. Close the emotional gap between where you are and what you want. Do that and what you want will arrive in your life. There might well come a time when the Old You will try to convince you that all of this is just too much effort: "Sod it! Let's watch telly. Who cares anyway, I'll never get it. I'm fine as I am. It's (I'm) not worth it." Ignore the

Old You. *Never* give up! You *are* worth it! You *are* amazing! You *can* do it!

- Frustration, stress and struggling are all resistance to what you really want. Notice them and replace them with your new vision of happiness. Worry or doubt about what you want just means that your vision isn't strong enough yet. Focus on building your vision. Do nothing until you are inspired to act from the strength of your vision.

- Basically, any time you are not feeling really good, you are resisting the good from coming to you. Any time you react negatively to anything that happens in your life is resistance. Unhappiness is the biggest resistance of them all. Begin with creating happiness and the resistance begins to fall away. Think of unhappiness as resistance to what you want, and when you notice it, lift yourself out of it because you now know what it is costing you— everything!

- It takes a lot of practice, but one day you will understand that you must only think about—focus on—what you want. Anything you give focus to, you allow to grow. Anything you allow to occupy your mind, creates feelings which create your reality. Ignore what you don't want, and focus solely on what you do want. This is the only way to allow the good into your life.

Magic ways to use visualisation in your daily life

- As the last thing you do at night, imagine you have just had the absolute best day ever. In your mind, reconstruct everything so that you came out on top. Relive the entire day with you as the hero to your story. Do this every day for a week and your life will never be the same.

- First thing in the morning, take five minutes to imagine how your day will go. Imagine that you are the hero of your story. If your day ahead panned out perfectly, what would it look like? What would it feel like? Create your life *on* purpose and *with* purpose. Otherwise Mr. Negativity will create it for you.

- Stop and take a breath before you walk through a door. Take a moment to decide how you want it to go on the other side. This could be getting home in the evening, arriving to work in the morning, going in to see the boss, going out on a date. Any time you are about to start something, take a breath and allow your imagination to become positive.

- Try the *Walk of Love*. Imagine a cartoon person who is in love. See how they walk in your mind's eye. See the bounce in their step, the swinging arms, the head moving from side to side. Hear the humming or whistling as they move down the street. They are the happiest people in the world. Now, I dare you to go out on the street and practise that walk. Pretend you have fallen in love with life itself. Act *as if*! That's all it is. When you do this often enough, one day you will wake up and realise you are no longer pretending.

- Imagine throwing all your troubles in a car, boat, or train and seeing them take off into the distance, getting smaller as they go. Then notice an express train screeching to a stop overflowing with solutions to everything!

- Imagine you have a protective shell around you keeping the positive in and the negative out.

- Imagine you know a wise man who knows everything and always gives you the answer you need at the perfect time.

- Just smile. For no reason, just do it. You will always feel better for it. But do it at the moment you least feel like it, and miracles will begin appearing in your life.

- Imagine you are the luckiest person in the world. Everything goes your way. How does that feel?

- If you feel tight in your stomach, imagine going inside and untying the knot.

- If you feel wound up, imagine going inside and unwinding the spring.

- If you feel stressed, imagine you are a bendy, flexible cartoon character.

- If you feel like you can't cope, imagine you are a super hero who takes on the World.

- If people get on your nerves, imagine you are the Buddha, and ask yourself what should I do now?

- Feeling blue? Imagine orange filling you up.

- Feeling gloomy? Imagine sunshine.

- Get fanciful yourself and create your own magical visualisations. The more fanciful you can imagine, the greater impact it will have on your subconscious.

How I stay positive

I mentioned earlier that I used to blandly read my affirmations twice a day with very little effect. Well, that was a long time ago now. I've since learnt that staying positive involves many winning habits throughout each and every day. Treat them as rituals—actions to be repeated over and over again.

- I do the "Walk of Love" at least once a day. It feels amazing. I get some funny looks because I really exaggerate it. But it's great fun.

- I collect those positive memes from Facebook and use them as my wallpaper. I stick with the subject of the moment, and then as I move on, I look for more suitable ones.

- I stick Post-it notes of encouragement all over the house.

- I listen to recordings of the great motivators: Jim Rhone, Les Brown, Rhonda Byrne, Jack Canfield. I listen to at least half an hour of somebody every day.

- I watch free motivational videos on YouTube (*People Are Amazing* is a favourite).

- I visualise my big vision for myself at least twice a day—bedtime and first thing in the morning.

- I visualise my next steps often throughout the day.

- I read books. Hundreds of books. Spiritual books, self-help books, business books. Anything positive that moves me forward or helps me grow.

- I study—business, coaching, writing, selling. Anything and everything I need to grow, be better, live a better life.

- I troll the Internet for free stuff. You can get it all now. Everything you could ask for. There are so many wonderful people out there who are giving away stuff for free. Whatever you want to be or do, you can find out how with a couple of clicks. You can build a boat from empty water bottles, build a house from wood, learn to coach, learn to teach, learn to surf or to paraglide, *anything*.

- I hang out with positive, successful people; whether in real life, or on the radio, on Facebook, in videos, audios, etc. You truly are influenced by the people you spend your time with. Hugely influenced.

- I give myself time to be alone with my thoughts. This is creation time and my most valuable time of all.

- I live a balanced life. Imagine a triangle. Each point represents each of the important areas of your life: work, rest and play. You are a dot in the middle of the triangle. Are you too close to any of the points? You should be maintaining a gentle little circle in the middle of the triangle at all times—never venturing too close to the points. A life in balance is a happy and peaceful life.

I do all these things all of the time. Staying positive takes *effort*. It is not enough to read quickly through your affirmations and think that's all you have to do for the day. The more you program yourself with positivity and think about what you want (visualise), the quicker you can have it. Focusing on what you *want* makes what you *don't want* fade away.

I am not saying that I am positive all the time. I don't even think that's possible. But the more I do these positive rituals, the more positive I feel, the more vivid my vision becomes, and the better my results get.

Remember, you get out what you put in, so put in lots, get out lots!

Make a greater commitment to yourself and you can live a greater life; and it all begins in your imagination.

Thank you

Thank you so much for reading my little book. I hope it serves you well and that you get everything you desire. If, after all this, you still have questions, just get in touch and ask away. I would love to hear from you, I really would, and I'll do my best to provide a suitable answer. Come and hang out with me on Facebook. Send me a friend request:

https://www.facebook.com/john.freeman.35977

Please take the time to add some feedback for the book. I know it's a pain in the arse, but your review really does make a huge difference.

When I'm not writing, I help successful people dramatically reduce their stress, regain control, cope easily and actually start enjoying their achievements.

For more information about myself and my work, please visit my website at:

http://johnfreeman-stressbuster.com/

Until Next Time...

Printed in Great Britain
by Amazon